WITH PERSONAL OKR AND PERSONAL KANBAN TO YOUR SUCCESS

USE LEADING METHODS FROM BUSINESS FOR YOUR PROFESSIONAL OR PRIVATE SUCCESS

PATRICK NIVEN

Contents

CHAPTER ONE

To the start

I am pleased to welcome you as a reader of this small guide to the successful use of OKR to achieve your own goals - professional or private.

OKR is a method developed at IBM for setting, tracking and achieving set goals. It has been continuously developed and is used by companies such as Google as an important basis for their success.

Kanban is used by leading global corporations in manufacturing environments, but also increasingly in knowledge-based processes to improve collaboration and goal achievement.

Now, you most likely don't own a global corporation and your goals might not be quite as extensive as Google's, for example. But that doesn't mean that you can't still have goals in life and that it's important to you to achieve them.

Let me start by asking you, before we get started here, do you actually have goals? Have you sat down quietly lately and thought about what you really want to achieve and how you can make it happen? Surprisingly few people really do this and tend to confuse goals with wishes that you say along the lines of: "I'd like to have that too", "I'd like to be there one day"...

Accordingly, let's do a little introductory exercise as a first step. Please take a few minutes and write down on a piece of paper your five[1] most important professional goals. If you are not interested in professional goals, you can of course also write down goals from another area of your life. However, try to focus on one area of life so that you don't get bogged down. Then, for each goal, note since when you have it (estimate if necessary), by when it should be implemented, and when (and how) you last consciously worked on realizing the goal. The whole thing could look like this:

Destination	Start date	When to reach?	Last conscious activity
Acquisition of a higher vocational qualification (part-time)	3.1.2022	5.1.2025	Participation in further training module "X

When I do this introductory exercise with course participants, I often find that many find it very difficult to write down their goals. Some realize that they have never really thought about it, others have far too many goals and can't decide what to write down. Sometimes, however, I experience people who find in this exercise that they have constantly changing goals and are not at all sure which direction to really go in. Sometimes goals seem to depend on the day, depending on what they have just experienced or what they have read or heard about. This not infrequently leads to the fact that eventually and finally no goal can be achieved at all.

It's a bit like you're driving on the highway, and depending on which truck you're passing, you'd adjust the destination each time. There's a truck coming from Hamburg and it's clear: Yes, I want to go to Hamburg! But a few dozen kilometers further on, you overtake a truck reading about the Bavarian Alps, and of course that would be something you'd really like to see! And so you turn around and drive south until you finally pass a truck of a flower dealer from the Netherlands and spontaneously decide that the tulip fields in the Netherlands might be quite interesting after all. Then, when you look out the window in the evening after a day behind the wheel, you realize to your astonishment that you are just passing the highway entrance where you entered the highway in the morning. Time and again I hear from people experiences that fit this image. They run around all day, exert themselves, do their really best, and yet have the impression that they not only get nowhere, but also always stay about the same distance from their destinations.

Too many goals, or goals that are spontaneously adjusted on an ongoing basis, lead to confusion. We get bogged down in many tasks, measures and activities and so it happens that instead of taking care of the important issues, we often spend the whole day implementing urgent things. Important tasks are often left until they become urgent or are forgotten behind the daily business. Due to the situation of having to meet many tasks and demands, we also realize again and again that things we have started are not finished because priorities have changed in between or a multitude of (other) urgent tasks have prevented us from implementing and completing what we really wanted to achieve.

This not only leads to us "not getting off the ground", but also has the effect of making us dissatisfied and demotivated, and in many cases this makes us even quicker to set new goals in order to "do something". So it also happens that even once we have achieved a goal, there is no satisfaction or sense of achievement. Because we are already thinking about the fact that there is a huge number of other goals waiting for us and that we haven't actually achieved anything yet.

Working with this publication, you will find ways for yourself to select the goals that are important to you from the mass of them, to work on them specifically, and to implement them. To do this, it is necessary that you not only read the information, but also implement the exercises yourself and actively work on them. This, by the way, is the most important reason why guidebooks often do not work: unfortunately, there is a large percentage of only readers of books and especially of guidebooks or similar books. However, success will never come from reading alone: So you won't lose weight if you stuff your face with French fries while reading a diet guide!

Make your investment in this book an investment in your future and take the first step towards achieving your goals by using this book as a workbook and implementing the content accordingly. Highlight things that seem important to you. Read up on things as needed and most importantly: get busy with the exercises and tasks. Only then will your investment in the purchase of this book have paid off and you will be significantly closer to realizing your goals.

But perhaps it is fundamentally difficult for you to formulate goals at all. Perhaps you don't have any goals because you gave up setting goals a long time ago or were unable to keep your goals in the past anyway. Unimplemented New Year's resolutions sometimes lead to these realizations. However, some people simply struggle with goal setting and wish someone would do it for them. Often this leads to such people being listless and empty. If there is no goal worth striving for: Then why and for what should I commit myself?

In the course of working with this text, you will learn how to find goals within yourself that seem worth striving for and how to realize them step by step. This will take effort. But when you see how you are gradually approaching your goals, you will find the necessary strength to do so. Because your own personal success will inspire you and move you forward step by step.

I also ask you to actively use this book and implement the tasks and exercises. If you don't want to do that, I suggest you give the book to someone who does. Just from reading it - or worse, just from having the book in a pile somewhere that you want to work through at some point - nothing will change in your life. But it is precisely in making a change that I want to support you, because that is what this book was written for.

If it wasn't particularly challenging for you to name specific goals, it could be that you are looking for a way to reliably achieve them. Perhaps you have already been successful in doing so and would simply like to improve your skills in this regard. Or perhaps you have stalled in setting goals and failed in implementing them, or at least experienced difficulties in doing so. Perhaps you have also put off the implementation and the measures necessary for it for a long time?

You, too, will find support in this book. Personal OKR is an approach that supports both the setting of goals and the implementation of the measures necessary to achieve them. Of course, it will also be of decisive importance for you that you not only read the book, but also do the exercises and implement the knowledge imparted.

[1] if you have more goals, decide on the five most important ones

CHAPTER TWO

OKR Knowledge

What are OKRs?

OKR stands for "Objectives and Key Results". We can translate Objectives as "goals" and Key Results as "important intermediate results". In combination, they form the core elements for our approach to setting and achieving goals.

An objective defines the final state of a change or development that I plan. That doesn't mean that there can't be further objectives after that. But we first focus on achieving this goal before we can tackle further steps. It is important to see clearly that an objective does not describe the way to the goal - or any activities we have to implement to reach the goal - but always describes the result. In other words, we record what the situation will be like when we have been successful and have achieved the goal. Completely open in this formulation of the objective remains the determination of the way, activities or means used to achieve this goal.

Examples could include:

- I am self-employed as a freelance photographer and make a stable living from this activity.
- I successfully completed the New York Marathon as one of the first 100 in my category.
- My contribution "..." is awarded in an international competition.

Even if some authors and trainers do not attach great importance to this: I have had very good experiences with goals being formulated in the "now" form as if they had already been achieved. In my experience, formulations such as "I would like to ...", "I will ..." etc. are not as strong and seem less concrete and thus provide less support.

You may have noticed from the wording that there is still a lot of ambiguity in it. On the one hand, nothing has been communicated about the way to realize the goal and, on the other hand, no specific point in time has been mentioned. The latter is usually not necessary in OKR practice, since in most cases you do OKR for a quarter. In some cases it is also used in the context of annual planning. In any case, the target date usually follows from the planning situation and therefore does not need to be specifically repeated in the individual target formulations. We also deliberately leave the path open in the formulation. If we were to name it already, we would possibly disregard a better way of achieving the goal that we have found. That would be counterproductive. However, we will deal with the path in more detail at a later stage.

Now we come to the second element, Key Results. In order to achieve a goal, it is necessary to perform certain activities. This is where Key Results come into play, which are not activities, but measurable steps/stages to achieve the goal.

This is precisely where the strength of OKRs becomes apparent. It is relatively easy to define goals, but if we leave it at that, there is a great risk that this abstract goal will never be achieved. If we really want to be successful, in addition to the objectives we have to record which essential steps we have to implement and achieve in order to reach our goal. We need to address these steps, monitor the corresponding activities and - if necessary - take appropriate action when obstacles arise.

There are some rules for the definition of such Key Results:

1. Key Results must be measurable by the person responsible for the OKR. They must be able to clearly identify and state whether or to what percentage a Key Result has been completed / not completed.
2. The responsible person must be able (opportunity/ability, resources) to pursue and achieve the Key Result.
3. Key Results must be achievable, but should always be challenging. Key Results should be defined so that they can be achieved within 3 months or less.
4. Three to four (no more, no less) key results are defined for each objective. If possible, the Key Results should be selected in such a way that the Objective has also been achieved when all of the Key Results have been realized.

Now you can see a very important point: If we state that Key Results should be completed within three months, and on the other hand we specify that the Objective should be realized when we have achieved the three to four Key Results, this would mean that only objectives which can be achieved within three months are suitable as Objectives. This would probably mean that some of the mentioned examples of objectives cannot be used in a really meaningful way. Depending on the level of training, it might be possible to participate in the New York Marathon, but even the idea of becoming a self-employed photographer is hardly feasible within one quarter, at least not if a large part of the process has not already been completed. Moreover, for such an extensive goal, one would probably have to define more than just three or four Key Results. However, this is not permissible.

It is also possible to define objectives that require more than three months for implementation. In such a case, you still define key results that can be achieved within one quarter. Once these are achieved, they are replaced by new key results, and this is continued until the major objectives are achieved. However, in my experience, this approach is not so attractive, because goals that can only be achieved in a very distant future often do not trigger the same attraction and motivation.

One approach I prefer here is to break down large objectives, which may only be achievable in a few years, into sub-objectives. The question would be something like this: If I want to have achieved X in three years, what do I have to have achieved by the end of the year or the end of the quarter? We will talk in more detail about working with such large objectives and structuring objectives across hierarchical levels at a later date. This approach offers the advantage that it is possible to regularly review the comprehensive objective, for example, when the "sub-objectives" are achieved, and to concretize or adjust them if necessary.

How to use OKRs to achieve goals

A central factor in achieving success is that we ourselves perceive progress toward our goals. Those who realize that they have already traveled part of the way to realization and can also measure this will draw further motivation from this, but will also take appropriate action if the desired successes fail to materialize. Achieving goals usually means an additional effort and in order to tackle them we depend on positive feedback. We need a sense of achievement. We achieve this by regularly measuring progress, because stagnation or progress that we do not perceive has a demotivating effect on us. Success, on the other hand, stimulates our motivation and our strength to continue working and thus to get closer to the realization of our goals.

Now let's look at the actions in chronological order:

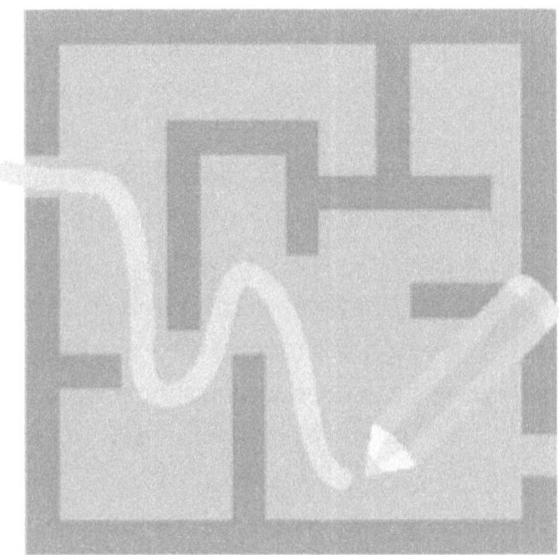

- **We start by** defining Objectives and Key Results and immediately begin working on their implementation.
- **Weekly**[1] take about five minutes to update the progress of the KRs. Record the percentage of achievement or whether the KR has already been achieved.
- **Each month,** you take about ten minutes of your time and again record the progress in the realization of the CRs and check whether any CRs have already been realized. Fulfilled KRs can be deleted and if it makes sense and is necessary, a new KR is created to achieve the objective.

- **Once a quarter,** we take a little more time (15-30 minutes). We have already talked about the fact that objectives should usually be achievable within one quarter. Accordingly, we now need to check their status. For each objective there are now two different procedures - depending on whether they are already fulfilled or not.

  - **If Objective fulfilled:** Celebrate your success. Don't just move on, but take some time to acknowledge your achievement. This will give you strength for the next goals. Define a new objective for each one you achieve.
  - **If the objective is not achieved:** If an objective is not achieved in the time that has elapsed, the question arises as to whether the objective can still be achieved at all and whether this is still meaningful. If this is not the case, the objective is cancelled and an attempt is made to learn lessons for the future from the failure. Subsequently, a new OKR is tackled. If the objective can still be fulfilled and makes sense, the associated CRs may have to be reviewed and adjusted if necessary. The entire objective may also have to be adjusted. Again, we should see what helpful experiences and lessons we can learn from this. These objectives will be further processed in the following quarter.

Note: This procedure is geared towards how you work with OKRs in the Personal OKR context. If you are working with OKRs in the context of an organization, the process is somewhat different, as this also involves several people in particular, and OKRs also need to be aligned and coordinated across several organizational levels.

Practical tips

- A little practical tip on the side: I have gotten into the habit of not simply writing down my KRs, but of writing them down on cards and pinning them to my wall: This is my personal "Wall of Fame", where I always notice what I have already achieved. From this I can draw a lot of strength for current and future efforts.
- As you can see, working with OKRs is not particularly complex. At least not their "administration". What matters much more are the actions to achieve the goals you set. But that depends on what kind of goals you set and how much effort is required to realize them. In any case, I recommend that you enter the OKR control dates in your electronic

agenda. Because as long as the work with OKR has not yet become a routine, these dates will otherwise be easily forgotten. As you have seen, the time required is manageable. Plan the time and do not allow yourself to simply postpone the appointment if it is not convenient at the moment. After all, this is an important appointment for the realization of your goals.

[1] Some authors also advise a frequency of 14 days; however, the shorter frequency leads to more focus and supports staying on the ball.

CHAPTER THREE

Achieving goals – mistakes and success factors

You probably already know these factors anyway. Nevertheless, let us briefly present the most important mistakes and success factors related to setting and achieving goals:

Goals are often confused with wishes. If you wish for something, you can make the wish and then leave it to someone else to fulfill it for you. The Christ Child, friends, whoever then has to take care of making your wish come true. You relinquish control and depend on the "wish granter." This is not what we mean when we talk about goals. Goals are clear ideas and a goal always includes an idea of how to achieve it.

An important attribute of good goals is that they are attractive to oneself. Goals which we tackle only to please others, because they are prescribed to us or because we believe that others expect us to achieve them, often have too little power and attraction for us to persevere. This is especially true when there is more effort involved in achieving them.

When we talk about a goal or several goals, they should always be a few, which we pursue at a given time. At a later point in time, when one goal has been achieved, you can tackle a new one. But if you work on too many goals in parallel, you will find that you don't really achieve any of them and only frustration remains.

However, this concrete idea of how to achieve the goal is not enough. Rather, the next step is to clearly plan the way to achieve the goal and to implement this plan. Only if this plan is realistic will it be feasible. So when creating the plan, always ask yourself: Is this realistic? Also, always keep in mind that you probably have other tasks and activities than just realizing the plan. If goals or plans are not perceived as realistic, we tend not to start in the first place: "What's the point of chasing a carrot when I know I'll never achieve it?"

Once the plan has been made, is perceived as realistic, and we set about implementing it based on the plan, the next important success factor is that we take some time regularly - ideally once a week at a fixed time - to determine how progress has been made toward implementation. Developments identified in this process support motivation, and if we find that we are not making progress toward a goal, we can address where adjustments are needed in the plan.

It happens again and again that framework conditions change: be it that the situation in the environment changes, be it that we ourselves change. A new relationship, a change of residence, the birth of a child, a career change, changes in the income situation or unforeseeable expenses are just a few aspects that can have a fundamental impact on our lives.

It is always a good idea to take a close look at whether the goals we have set ourselves are still achievable or whether they are no longer feasible. It may be necessary to make adjustments here. However, this should be solidly justified in order not to fall into the trap of many aborted plans.

I often see people who give up far too quickly. They realize that they haven't reached their goal yet, or they don't find the progress towards achieving the goal sufficient, suspect that they can't reach the goal anyway, and throw in the towel. How long is the chain of your goal-achievement projects that have been abandoned in this way? I admit mine is very long and it is only since I have been working in a concentrated way with Personal OKRs that I am gradually getting closer and closer to my goals and for the most part achieving them.

Then, when a goal is achieved, you should celebrate it. Reward yourself. Do something good for yourself. Give yourself recognition. Too often we take the achievement of a goal for granted. In doing so, we withhold reward from ourselves, which affects our strength to tackle new goals. We need a sense of achievement to be successful. If we do not perceive them or hardly perceive them at all, the effort required to achieve further goals is all the greater.

CHAPTER FOUR

Successful with your personal OKRs

Now let's start working on defining and implementing your personal goals. It does not matter whether these goals concern your personal life, your professional life or possibly other aspects of your life.

Step 1: What do you want to achieve?

First, I recommend that you get an overview of your goals. You may have a few that come to mind right away. But are they the right ones, the ones that are sufficiently attractive and important to you that you will work on realizing them, or are they possibly just wishes that are current at the moment? Keep a record of your goals. You may have already recorded a few of them in the initial exercise, and if you give yourself some time, for example, sleep on them, other goals may come to mind that were no longer present in the hustle and bustle of everyday life.

Take the time and hold on to all your ideas, even if they may seem "not the right ones" at first glance. My experience shows that the really important goals are sometimes a little less present in the confusion of everyday life, and if you take the time to trace them, the more important and clearer goals are often recognized. In this way, we also want to counter the frequently occurring phenomenon that there are so many ideas and conceptions of goals that you want to change them permanently because somehow none of them seems to fit quite right.

Step 2: Make your selection

Now make your selection from the list. Choose the three destinations that excite you the most / have the greatest appeal to you. If there are more than three that you are attracted to, still limit your selection to three. If the objectives are too big to be achieved within 3 months, formulate an objective that represents an intermediate goal and brings you a significant step closer to your "big goal". Keep the "big goal" as a strategic objective and do not lose sight of it. However, for the next steps, work with the less comprehensive objective, which is the first step toward the strategic goal. Strategic Objectives should generally be achievable within 12 months. Once you've achieved the first one, you can always tackle another. However, if you pursue too many parallel goals, you risk not achieving any at all in the end because you get bogged down and overestimate your strength.

Record the goals and formulate them as if they had been achieved. By doing so, you describe the target state that attracts you so much and thus avoid falling into the trap of visualizing and implementing the path or solution approach instead of the target. In doing so, however, the path may not be so attractive, but may include activities that are not quite so attractive.

You have now set your first three Objectives.

Step 3: The Key Results

For each of the three defined objectives, record three to four key results that bring you closer to your goal. Ideally, the objective is achieved when the three to four key results are achieved. Sometimes, however, more are needed. Nevertheless, limit yourself to three to four Key Results. Again, the power is in the focus. You can remember three to four Key Results and integrate their implementation into your daily routine. If, on the other hand, you write down more Key Results, you run the risk of forgetting something or diverting your energy to too many tasks and experiencing frustration because the whole project does not seem to be progressing.

Step 4: Create transparency

Goals are not realized by writing them down somewhere, but by constantly confronting them and working on them. Therefore, print out your OKRs and hang them somewhere where you can see them again and again (at least once in the morning and once in the evening). You can also set them up as a screen saver on your laptop or put them as a wallpaper for your smartphone or tablet so you will always be reminded of them.

It helped me a lot when I started to change the position of the prints from time to time as well, or add any other variations. In this way, you reduce the risk of the OKRs simply becoming part of the setup over time and being overlooked.

I also started talking to some very close friends about the OKRs, and I have been asked about it from time to time since then, how the progress is. That can also be a help - but you should decide that for yourself. Last but not least, it may also depend on the nature of your goals, how far you can and want to communicate them to third parties.

Another possibility is that you deliberately choose a picture that symbolizes for you the goal you have achieved. For example, hang this picture up in your office or put it there if you don't want anyone else to be able to read the goal. This way, only you know what the picture means and what statement is behind it.

Step 5: Progress check

Set a weekly recurring appointment that you define in your calendar. It is of maximum importance and should only be postponed in extreme emergencies. In this appointment, deal with each of your Key Results. What did you do to achieve them? What have you achieved with them? Record the progress. This can be done on paper, in a program like Excel®, a special OKR tool or similar. Since I also often work with GoodNotes on my iPad, I have created a separate notebook for this in GoodNotes[1] , where all my OKR topics are located and which is also synchronized by GoodNotes across my various devices such as iPhone, Mac Powerbook, iPad. So I always have access to it. Of course, such things can also be done with other appropriate platforms. Originally I had used Microsoft OneNote for this, but then I was quickly convinced of the advantages of GoodNotes.

I have already written in more detail about this weekly progress check.

Step 6: Quarterly review

Set a quarterly deadline and do the quarterly review described earlier. When you have achieved an objective, take the time to celebrate it. Recognition, also towards yourself and your own achievements, is an enormous source of strength, which you can use as a basis for your further development. If Key Results have been achieved that are not yet sufficient to ensure that the Objective has also been achieved, set new Key Results - with the aim of achieving the Objective in the coming quarter if possible by realizing the Key Results or at least getting significantly closer to this goal. In your work with the Objectives and Key Results, always focus on the successes. Issues where the desired goals were not achieved should not be interpreted as failures, but rather as a basis for questioning your procedures and goals. This will provide you with a good basis for your personal development.

[2]

Checklist for your implementation

Hopefully, you have now formulated your first OKRs. Let's make sure together that you are on the right track. Below I have compiled a checklist which should help you to find errors in the structure, if any have occurred. I recommend that you refer to this list in the future when you develop new OKRs to ensure that nothing is forgotten and that you do not overextend yourself in your enthusiasm.

◯

I have defined no more than four Objectives (better 3) at a time.

◯

The objectives are defined in such a way that I can achieve them within 3 months (1 quarter). Strategic objectives are defined so that they can be achieved within one year.

○

I have defined 3-4 Key Results per Objective.

○

All Key Results are clearly measurable in terms of their degree of completion. Measures can be percent (%), yes/no, x of y implemented (e.g. 7 of 10)

○

I have the OKRs displayed (hung, set up as background or similar) so that I see them several times a day.

○

I have a date set in my agenda for the weekly progress check.

○

I have defined a place where progress is recorded. (Paper, Excel, Application ...)

○

I have defined a date for the quarterly review and put it in my agenda.

○

The objectives and key results are challenging, attractive and worth my work. They make me leave my comfort zone and also develop as a person.

You see, the whole thing is not really difficult. It's a bit like making good New Year's resolutions. You're probably familiar with this: Good intentions are not enough. Now it's time to put them into practice, and in the process you'll have to bite your way through from time to time and fight the inner bastard who tries to convince you that you could be doing something completely different "right now" and that the work on realizing your goals "has time".

An example

Let's tackle a concrete example. In the context of Corona and the associated changes in the economy with home office, short-time work, etc., many people have begun to consider the idea of self-employment or have already taken the first steps toward implementation. So let's take an example from this context.

Accordingly, the goal could be formulated as follows: "I am successful with my business "X" and can live well from the income it generates."

If you already have some experience with setting goals, you may have noticed that this formulation is still very fuzzy. It's worth questioning it a little more closely. A few questions to ask might be:

- What does "successful" mean to me?
- How much turnover / profit do I need to make each month in order to be able to live "well" on the income generated and also to be able to put aside enough money to survive fluctuations?
- What do I do when I reach the goal?
- What have I already achieved so far in terms of realizing the goal?
- ...

As you can see: There is still a lot that needs to be clarified and that may not be answered so easily and quickly. So it might be a good idea to clarify these questions in detail first. To do this, it may also be necessary to consult with a tax advisor or other experts on certain topics. This does not mean that we must now stop working on our business. It's just a matter of putting our activities on a solid footing right from the start. For example, we should formulate a goal like the following as our first quarterly target:

- "I know what conditions and framework I need to create in order to be able to live successfully and financially independently with my Business X. "

Now you could formulate two more Objectives, which will bring you closer to your "big goal". Examples are:

- "I have updated my knowledge on the subject of XYZ and am familiar with the techniques and processes currently used in the industry."
- "I discussed my plans with the family and worked with them to make an implementation plan that they agreed with."

Key Results matching the first Objective:

Be sure to record actual results, not the path to them. Often Key Results are described as activities such as "Create all ..." or "Develop ...". Again, focus on what the outcome of the activities should be - i.e., not "I am developing a business plan for the first three years," but "A business plan for the first three years exists and has been deemed realistic by my tax advisor." Stick to the rule of 3 to 4 Key Results per Objective. Another example of the first Objective: "I have an overview of my current financial resources, taking into account all asset classes, and know what funds I have available for my venture."

You see: These are all doable results and you can continuously assess how far you have already implemented them. When one of them is achieved, you will formulate further Key Results, if necessary, if there is still something to do to realize your Objective.

Once you have achieved the first objective, you can return to the originally formulated goal: "I am successful with my business "X" and can live well from the revenues it generates." Possibly, based on your findings, you will be able to become more concrete with the business case and thereby derive better Key Results for implementation. Of course, realizing your goal of becoming successful with business "X" may take more than one quarter. This even seems to be quite realistic. Then it makes sense to formulate another goal for the next quarter, which can be realized within the time available and brings you a good step closer to your actual goal. Nevertheless, this goal is valuable for you. It is your source of motivation. It's what you're doing it for. It provides you with an appropriate incentive.

You can support this source of motivation by painting as attractive and colorful a picture as possible of what their success should look like. You can do this by drawing, but you can also make collages, for example with pictures from newspapers or magazines. The more you engage and identify with the goal, the more it will motivate you. Hang the picture so that you see it as often as possible.

[1] https://www.goodnotes.com/

[2] Image license: elements.envato.com

CHAPTER FIVE

Different types of KRs

There are various approaches to the use of OKRs. One approach, strongly advocated by John Doerr and Google, is to set very ambitious key results. Key results are considered to be well formulated if they can be achieved by 70%. Accordingly, an achievement level of 70% is already considered a success (some organizations also work with 60%). If 100% of the Key Results are achieved, there is a perception that the targets have not been set ambitiously enough.

Such an approach not only contradicts all common approaches to goal setting, but also does not fit with our own need to want to conclude things. That's exactly the point, too. These goals strive to draw us out of our comfort zone and inspire us to "go the extra mile." People tend to set goals that they feel are safely achievable. However, these are also goals that do not challenge us in any particular way and tend not to require us to leave our comfort zone, thus preventing further development.

Google deliberately demands key results that are actually not achievable. This leads to the fact that you have to make a special effort and think of new ways to master the requirements anyway. However, this type of Key Results should not be tackled right at the beginning. First, take some time to gain experience with the OKR approach, which is new to you, and to familiarize yourself with the basic approach. Often, setting goals that we think are only 60-70% achievable goes against our perfectionism and everything we were taught in our school days. You might also wonder how you can get any motivation at all from a challenge that you don't think is achievable anyway.

Especially when starting with OKR, these fears are absolutely understandable. Especially if you introduce OKR in a professional environment where employees are used to the fact that the achievement of a target is possibly linked to the achievement of a bonus or variable salary components. Accordingly, a company will not immediately recommend or implement such targets when introducing OKRs, but will give all parties involved - employees as well as supervisors and management - sufficient opportunity to gain experience.

Only when the approach has been practiced and initial successes have been achieved should you consider taking this further step toward more ambitious key results. However, you should always keep in mind that despite all the enthusiasm for further development, "daily business" must also continue. It's no use being extremely innovative and constantly releasing new products if we don't manage to market what we have developed and bring it to the customer. So, in most cases, it will probably make sense to set a mix of different types of goals. To this end, a distinction is often made between "ambitious goals" and "must-do" goals (also called committee goals). In this context, we naturally assume that, unlike ambitious targets, must targets must also be achieved 100% in order to be considered successful.

But why now two types of goals? Basically, the distinction between must-have goals and ambitious goals also means that we can place a strong focus on the must-have goals. These absolutely must be achieved, whereas with the ambitious goals we assume that we will not achieve them 100% (but of course do our best to do so anyway). In this way, we ensure that not all resources are spent on the realization of ambitious goals and that, as a result, a must-achieve goal falls by the wayside, which can possibly lead to the project as a whole being called into question.

Finally, to ensure the basics or day-to-day operations or the like, you will generally combine 1-3 must-have goals with 1-2 ambitious OKRs. Now, if we look at this using our example, it may well make sense that you will formulate one to three must-do goals in the context of your existing self-employment activities. These will ensure that what you have already achieved is also secured and, if necessary, still stabilized, and that you lay the foundations for further development. In addition, you should formulate one to two further goals, which are aimed at bringing you closer to the goal of self-employment with your project.

CHAPTER SIX

Personal Kanban

One might wonder what a larger section on Personal Kanban is doing in a book on Personal OKR. In fact, this combination has emerged in my own efforts, even though both methods in themselves have nothing directly to do with each other, except that they both come from the broad field of modern working methods and frameworks.

In my own implementation of OKR, I noticed at the beginning that setting goals with OKR was a lot of fun and also led to a lot of motivation to achieve the goals, but that the implementation was quite demanding. In addition, for me, as possibly for you, there were goals that did not arise within the framework of my "normal activity" anyway and simply channeled it a little further, but it was about additional work, which then began to compete with the multitude of other tasks in everyday life.

Perhaps you know this too? In normal everyday life, the urgent tasks often fight with the important ones about what should be worked on now. Some tasks you probably set yourself. These include, for example, household chores, perhaps activities to support your fitness and health, and many others. In addition, there may be family and loved ones who also require effort. In addition, there may be tasks from the professional environment. Perhaps you are also active in a club or are continuing your education? All these different areas - and often many more - compete for the 24 hours that are available to you during the day, and in addition you probably also have the need to sleep, eat or rest. So it's easy for something to get left behind. It was like that with me, at least in the beginning. I realized relatively soon that I couldn't get off the ground with my goals because so many other, urgent things held my attention captive. I looked for a remedy and found it with the very simple Personal Kanban. This approach in combination with Personal OKR has resulted in me safely achieving many of my goals and making very good progress on the current goals I have set for myself and am confident that I can achieve them as well.

But what is Personal Kanban actually?

Basics of Personal Kanban

Personal Kanban is a further development of Kanban for the organization of the own work. There are extensions based on it, in order to use Personal Kanban also in larger context of several persons. However, I would like to focus here on the area where it is about using your own time better - and above all more purposefully. More precisely: I would like to focus on how you can significantly increase the probability of actually achieving your goals (Objectives) with Personal Kanban.

We all have a variety of tasks, as outlined earlier. Some of them are extremely important, others are particularly urgent, some are both. Some things we do even though they are neither one nor the other, simply because we "stumble over them" and don't even think about whether the time we need to realize the task is well spent. Often we have so many tasks going on at the same time that we start to get bogged down. Friends, superiors, family members, neighbors and many others ask us to do something for them, and of course we say "yes" and then at some point we realize that the work is getting on top of us and we get stressed. For some people, this takes on such extreme features that they permanently damage their health and react with symptoms such as burnout, stomach complaints, sleep disorders or heart disease.

The background to this is often the excess of tasks. This results in the situation that we can never really be successful, but rush from one task to the next, forgetting some, not finishing some, or if we finish them, not doing it in the quality that is expected. This, in turn, leads us to another task: to fix the mistakes that have been made. Especially self-set tasks and goals are often lost, because no one asks and no one is angry with us if we do not implement them in time. But this way we will never reach our objectives.

Personal Kanban is based on two very simple basic principles. First, it is about gaining an overview of all existing tasks. This is related to the fact that we also prioritize them accordingly. What is important, what is urgent, what is unimportant ... Then it is about planning our own time, limiting the number of tasks we work on in parallel, so that we can fully concentrate on a few things in the time available. Only when something has been completed should a new task be tackled. So far once the completely fundamental concept of personal Kanban. But as always: In practice there are many questions and topics, which it more exactly to consider applies, in order to obtain with this extremely helpful method also the desired successes. We now want to take a closer look at this.

Implementation 1: Your open tasks

The good thing about using Personal Kanban in the context of OKR is that it is not a method that focuses on the implementation of OKR, but Personal Kanban is designed to help you implement your tasks - regardless of the context they come from. In fact, it would even be a hindrance if you only recorded your tasks in the context of OKR.

In your life, tasks arise in a wide variety of contexts. Some are brought to you by others, such as superiors. Other tasks you set for yourself, or they arise from the promise of requests and inquiries from friends, family members, or others. All of these tasks are in constant competition for your time. This is limited. Even if you did not sleep, more than twenty-four hours per day would not be available for completing tasks.

Therefore, take the time to work on the following implementation task before reading the other chapters. This book is only helpful if you put into practice the things you learn. Many people forget this and are proud of the number of books they have read. The important question is: What have you implemented from the books you have read? Because only what you actually implement will bring you further. This applies to your goals as well as to everyday topics and tasks.

The first step we take when we get to grips with Kanban is to start writing down all the tasks that we cannot implement immediately on sticky notes. These have the advantage that we can move them around as we work and they still retain their stickiness. You should only record one task per sticky note. If you have tasks that consist of several parts that can also be implemented individually, you can also record them separately.

For example, if you are preparing for a final exam with different subjects, it may make sense to record the individual subjects as separate cards. In time, you may even find that it makes sense to record individual chapters or topics per subject. But for now, just start as it suits you. You can also adjust everything at a later stage if it seems to make sense to you.

So start recording what comes to your mind. Take some time to do this and don't put yourself under pressure. If you forget something, you can always add it later. While you are working, do not forget those tasks that you have undertaken in connection with the realization of your OKRs.

You have probably gathered a large amount of tasks. Some are more extensive, some are relatively simple and can be done quickly. Some are urgent and others have time. Did you even have an overview of all the open tasks or could it be that now and then you simply forgot about tasks or implemented them too late?

Now please do not make the mistake of starting with all the tasks. Read a little further first. We will deal with the tasks, the flow of work and the limitation of started work.

As a little preliminary work, however, you could briefly divide your tasks on the sticky notes into the following categories. You can do this, for example, by writing four boxes with the four different categories on a large piece of wrapping paper and sticking the respective sticky notes in one of the boxes.

The four categories:

- **Important**: Things that are important to you; this could include tasks related to your OKRs, but possibly several others as well.
- **Urgent**: Things that have a completion date that is within the next few days.
- **Important AND Urgent**: Cards that fall into both of the above categories: that is, both important and urgent.
- **Other**: Sticky notes with tasks that do not belong in any of the three aforementioned boxes.

Important means "important for you" - but there may also be tasks that are only indirectly important for you, for example, because they are important for a close person whom you do not want to disappoint or whom you want to support, or because it is important for your employer, for example, and you have to do it as part of your job.

If you now have tasks which are in the "Other" category, ask yourself why you want to spend energy and time on their implementation. Would it possibly make sense to simply complete these tasks or "return them to sender"? In some cases, that may work. But there may also be tasks that are not important or urgent right now, but will become so at some point. If you are not sure about a task, leave it in this area for the time being. But what you can remove with a calm heart, you should get rid of. All the tasks on the slips of paper are competing for a very rare and valuable resource: your time.

To that end, I have a tool for you that a very busy man, former U.S. President Dwight D. Eisenhower, developed for himself.

The Eisenhower Principle

Dwight D. Eisenhower was President of the United States from 1953 to 1961. Before that, he served as a general in the U.S. Army and as Commander-in-Chief of the Allied Forces during World War II, and later he also became the first Commander-in-Chief of NATO.

He faced the challenge of constantly making difficult decisions about which of many tasks to focus on. As a tool, he developed the Eisenhower Principle, which still helps us today to prioritize according to urgency and importance.

Tasks are classified according to urgency and importance in a matrix.

Urgent (today/tomorrow)	**(3) Delegate**	**(1) Do it immediately**
Not urgent (later)	**(4) Strike / Trash**	**(2) Schedule completion**
	unimportant	important

- I have labeled the first quadrant "**Do Now**" because its tasks are important to your life, career, or in some other context and must be done today or tomorrow at the latest. You should tackle these tasks with high importance and urgency first. An example could be that you have received an important and urgent assignment from your supervisor as part of your job.
- I have titled the second quadrant "**Schedule Completion**". The tasks included are important, but less urgent. Here you should list tasks that you need to schedule at the right time. It can be helpful to note the completion date you need to meet on the card. An example here might be implementing activities related to your OKRs. These are not scheduled to be implemented the following day. We generally set a timeframe of a quarter for these (which of course doesn't mean we should only tackle implementation in the last days of the quarter), but they are no less important because of that.
- I have labeled the third quadrant "**Delegate**". These are tasks that are urgent, but from your point of view do not have the corresponding importance. Often we have such tasks piling up. Perhaps you have always

taken over all of them and invested a lot of time in their completion, while afterwards the time was missing for other tasks. If possible, you should delegate such tasks or not accept them at all. It is always difficult to say "no" to a request. But if saying "yes" means that you can't perform more important tasks properly or on time, then it's certainly worth communicating clearly here.

- I have overwritten the contents of the last quadrant with "**Delete**" or "**Trash**". This refers to everything that is not important and not urgent. Why should you spend valuable energy and time on it, which you might then miss on important tasks? Many of us have a huge potential in this category to manage our time better. In fact, it often takes time and experience to get rid of such tasks or not to take them on in the first place.

Look through your tasks again, which you have recorded, and decide what you want to focus on. Decide what goes into the "delegate" quadrant. What is urgent, but not important, you should look at more closely. Where is the opportunity to delegate such work?

Visualize the flow of work and limit the work started

Now let's get back to the gray theory. The two basic principles of Personal Kanban are: "**Visualize the flow of work**" and "**Limit the work started**".

Visualize the workflow

The first step in visualization is to gain an overview of the open tasks. You have just started with this in the implementation exercise. The visualization in Personal Kanban is primarily based on a simple board that contains three columns: "Ready" (also called "Backlog" or "To Do") "In Progress" (or "Doing") and "Done".

Ready / Backlog / To Do	In progress / Doing	Done / Done

In Kanban approaches in a larger environment, we would probably subdivide the "In progress" column into further sub-processes. For our purposes, however, the list is sufficient for the time being, especially since we do not follow a fixed process flow, but work on a variety of different tasks.

Open tasks are now placed in the "Ready" column. Here, too, there is the possibility that we insert additional columns with "Worklist" or similar and then only put the tasks that we want to tackle next in "Ready". Overall, Personal Kanban, like Kanban itself, is not very rule-driven. While rules are an important foundation to give us some structure and direction, there is always the possibility to adjust rules or procedures as well, if we find it useful and purposeful to do so.

So now we have a column titled "Ready" and you can put the sticky notes you created in implementation exercise 1 there.

Can it be that the multitude of tasks in the column somewhat "overwhelms" you and you have the feeling of being overwhelmed by their sheer number? This happens quite often and so it is important that you do not see this "Ready" column as a kind of "task list" which you have to work through until the last task. Rather, you should see the list as a transparent overview that allows you to make clear decisions about what you are working on (and thus using your very scarce resource of "time") and where you decide not to tackle a task.

The goal here is to ensure that you use your time more purposefully and - instead of starting dozens of tasks - focus on completing things. As a small decision-making tool and example of a possible approach, we've divided tasks into different categories in the implementation exercise. For new tasks that you set for yourself or that are set for you by others, always ask yourself into which category this task belongs.

This gives you a first basis for deciding whether to accept the task or not. Furthermore, this is a good basis for prioritization in the "Ready" or "Backlog" column. Tasks with higher priority are placed further up in the column, those with lower priority further down. You can make this very sophisticated by comparing two tasks at a time. What has higher priority goes to the top, what has lower priority goes to the bottom. This way you can display a whole sequence, which can be taken into account later in the implementation. New entries are sorted by priority: either under a more important task or above, if the new task has a higher priority.

In addition to the purely factual justification of a prioritization, however, personal aspects should not be neglected. Which tasks do you enjoy, which ones perhaps less? You can also include this aspect in your prioritization. If you constantly have to do things that you don't enjoy or, in the worst case, that you deeply dislike, this will affect your motivation. You will probably be less productive than if, in between less attractive tasks, you can occasionally do things that you really enjoy and which thus provide energy for further activities.

In Kanban there is the maxim "Stop starting, start finishing" - i.e. the clear challenge to put the emphasis on finishing tasks. To start work and to work on it means from the point of view of Kanban simply use of resources - so to speak accumulation of costs. It is only through the completion of work that benefits are created and thus, in accounting terms, a "return". Instead of somehow keeping a hundred tasks in progress and thus generating enormous amounts of effort and draining your resources, we now focus on completing tasks, and it is in this context that the second Personal Kanban principle in particular: "Limit the work you have started. "

Limit the work you have started

So far we have talked about the first column of the Kanban board. We have overwritten it with "Ready" or "Backlog". Now we want to deal with the second column. We'll label this one "In Progress" or "Doing". If you take a closer look at your tasks, it could very well be that a large number of cards, which we have parked in the first column so far, should actually have been in the second column long ago, because you have already started working on them. It could be that quite a few of the tasks have been worked on for a very long time and have continuously had to take a back seat to new, more urgent ones. Maybe you even found out during your work with the goals that you suddenly remembered work you had started, which was long forgotten or maybe already overdue?

Let's make a simple calculation: For the sake of simplicity, let's assume that you have ten hours per day to work on your tasks. Let's also assume, somewhat exaggeratedly, that you are working on twenty-five tasks at the same time, all of which you have already started but not yet completed. The calculation is relatively simple: Per task you would have an average of 10 hours / 25 tasks = 0.4 hours or 24 minutes. There is not much you can finish. Now imagine in our model that you have only 3 tasks in progress and that you start a new task only after you have completed one of them. You would then have an average of 3 ⅓ hours, or 200 minutes, per task. This would significantly increase the likelihood of completing things in a timely manner, and then when you have completed a task, you could decide which task to tackle next. This is exactly the central goal of what we mean by "limit the work you start." We want to make sure that we can focus on a few tasks instead of working on a confusing number. This will significantly reduce the turnaround time, that is, the time that exists between the start of work and its completion, while maintaining the same workload.

On the one hand, this offers the advantage that we also achieve a sense of achievement by completing tasks and thus have more motivation at work, and on the other hand, it also means that we are better able to keep our promises and thus in turn also receive more recognition from outside.

So we try to get by with as little parallel work as possible, because we know that every task change, i.e. every change between different tasks - apart from the fact that the work which has now not been completed remains lying around again for longer - produces additional effort due to the change of focus. Maybe you know this as well: You were just highly concentrated on a task. Suddenly the phone rings and you are distracted and devote your attention to the call. Afterwards, you have to get your bearings again and see where you were and what you wanted to do. Maybe you had a creative idea for a solution or you just thought of a possible problem before the phone rang and now it just doesn't occur to you anymore? This change in focus is extremely draining and leads to an overall loss of quality and performance. So the best approach would be: you work on one task at a time and only when it's completed do you start the next one. By eliminating the extra effort of switching, you can already get significantly more done without any additional work than you would in a multi-task environment.

The important thing is that it is always you who decides what to do next, and only pull new tasks into processing when there is appropriate capacity there.

In the context of your implementation, I would recommend that you do not drag all tasks into the middle column and implement them accordingly, but only a manageable number that you can also complete in a short time: a maximum of three is ideal for getting started. We also talk about a WIP limit, where WIP stands for Work in Progress[1] . Based on your experience, you may be able to adjust the number over time.

Now it may be that a client, for example a supervisor, suddenly stands with a task from you that must be implemented immediately. How can you deal with this if the limit you set yourself has already been reached? At least you can now make transparent to your client what you are currently working on. This can lead to a discussion about which task is now more important, and perhaps this can lead to him withdrawing the task or insisting that you bring his task forward. This is in line with the idea of transparency, which is very important in all agile approaches, because it allows to look for a better way with each other and to make the best possible decisions based on facts.

In concrete terms, therefore, different situations can now arise:

- The client agrees with your assessment and asks you to tackle the task as soon as the current tasks in progress are completed.
- Nevertheless, the client asks you to bring forward his task. In that case, I would advise you to complete this task as soon as possible and put the other tasks in progress on hold until after the "special task" has been implemented, thus returning to your WIP limit, i.e. to your set number of tasks in progress.

Let's go back to our Kanban board. When we have completed a task, we will move the corresponding slip of paper into the third column of the Kanban board. This third column is headed with "Finished", "Done" or comparable texts as already shown.

But why is this completed work now pushed
into another column at all? We could simply throw away the corresponding piece of paper. After all, the associated work is done.

Retrospectives / Kaizen

Completed work is shown in a separate column in Personal Kanban (and also in other agile methods like Kanban or Scrum). This has a simple reason. If we simply throw away completed task descriptions, there is a risk that we will quite soon lose track of what we have all done and simply forget certain tasks.

Now, one could say that this is not a problem. If the task is completed, we have done our duty and we will probably not receive any inquiries from third parties asking about the whereabouts of the task. This is an issue, however, when we are required to provide a report on completed tasks, for example. This can happen when we are supposed to give a work list to a supervisor or charge a customer for services or, as part of a team, inform colleagues about what is ready for further processing.

However, there is a second aspect, which is much more important from an agile point of view, which makes it useful to record completed work. It is about an activity, which is often called retrospective or kaizen in the technical literature. This activity is about the topic of "continuous improvement".

You will undoubtedly find in the course of your work that various tasks have been completed, but that progress may have been slow. Maybe there were mistakes, maybe there were misunderstandings, or maybe you had to start things from scratch because you got lost somewhere. These are undoubtedly unpleasant experiences, but everyone has them in one way or another. But if you just move on and are glad that you "finally got the crap done", you will probably fall into the same trap again in a similar case and make a similar mistake. This is exactly where it makes sense if we regularly - for example every evening or once a week - look back on our tasks and briefly consider what went well with each completed task and where mistakes may have occurred or could just be worked around. Of course, the next step would then be to ask what can be learned from this and what can be approached differently - better - in the future.

This is exactly one of the key success factors of agile approaches, such as (Personal) Kanban or (Personal) OKR! Agile work always assumes that we question our procedures and look for opportunities for improvement. These are rarely huge steps, but changes that we can tackle in small steps - similar to OKR. They are meant to help us work better. Better can mean: "better quality achieved", "worked more effectively", "had more fun at work", "worked better with others", "implemented things more purposefully" ... The decision is yours alone.

Now that you have the overview of the completed work, you can ask yourself such questions for each of the works and ideally derive one or two concrete improvement measures from them. In doing so, it may well be that these measures also include the risk that things will not work as you might want them to. So it will be a matter of evaluating the measure in a further retrospective - when you have tried the new approach for some time and have thus completed things. If it led to improvements in the aspect you defined, you should keep the new course of action. If it was not successful, you can decide whether the action was good but you need more practice, or whether you should discard the action and look for an alternative.

Last but not least, another important aspect of the "Done" or "Finished" column is also that it gives you the opportunity to notice what you have done and also congratulate yourself for it and also celebrate these achievements. There is no doubt that you deserve it.

Checklist: Create your own Personal Kanban Board

You have probably already worked on your own Personal Kanban Board over the course of the last few sections. Let's take a closer look at the different steps again. For this purpose, I have compiled a checklist for you below. If you have not started with the board yet, take the checklist as a guide through the process and build your board. Very importantly, what I present to you is not "set in stone truth". An important part of Kanban and also Personal Kanban is that you can start very low-threshold where you are right now. So if your board looks different, there is nothing wrong with that. You can start with what you have and if you find that it works fine the way you are doing it and you are progressing well, you have already achieved a lot. Nevertheless, even then you should always look back at the work you have done and consider how you can make the process of your work even better. What "better" means is up to you. In this context, you can, if you wish, also check the aspects in the checklist and, where it seems sensible to you, adjust your process accordingly.

Prepare the board

An obvious first step is to create a board. You can work with physical boards like whiteboards, pinboards, flipcharts, simple walls, refrigerator doors, etc., but also with boards like Trello or one of the many providers that offer their boards as an app or online platform. , but also with boards such as Trello or one of the many other providers that offer their boards as an app or online platform. Important for the choice is that the board is visible and easily accessible for you in everyday life, so that you can update changes, such as completed work packages, at any time. Hardly anything is more pointless than a plan with outdated data.

Determine the value stream

So far, we have worked with a very simple value stream representation. We will talk in the further sections about whether and to what extent extensions can be useful both in terms of the number of process steps and in terms of distinguishing between different types of tasks. The simplest representation simply includes "Ready," "To Do," or "Backlog" as the first column, "In Progress" or "Doing" as the second column, and "Done" or "Done" in a final column. This basic pattern will remain as we continue to expand. However, it may be, for example, that we decide to subdivide the "In Work" step into further sub-steps or, if necessary, we will also implement further work steps that distinguish different types of open tasks according to certain aspects.

Create the backlog

Fill your personal backlog. Don't wait for the backlog to be "full" before continuing work. The list will constantly adapt. Be it because new tasks arise, be it because tasks are changed in their prioritization or possibly even dropped again.

Prioritization will be easiest if you directly enter the entries in the backlog in the order that suits you. If a new entry is added, you can place it in the appropriate place in the sequence based on "more important than X" or "less important than Y". It is common to put the tasks with the highest priority at the top.

Attention: New insights or new input (for example from the supervisor or similar) can change priorities and thus also sequences.

Setting the WIP limit

Now it is necessary to determine how many work packages (tasks) are to be worked on in parallel. The point is to maintain focus and not get bogged down in implementation. The more things you work on in parallel, the more time it will take on average to implement the tasks. A good value to start with is "3". Based on your experience, you can always adjust it. Do not fall into the pattern of wanting to work on everything in parallel!

As far as possible, keep a written record of theset WIP limit, i.e. the number of tasks that should be in the "In progress" column in parallel.

Implement tasks

Based on your prioritization, you now tackle tasks. Limit the number to the number set in the WIP limit.

Only when a task is completely done do you drag a new task, again based on the current prioritization, into the "In Work" column and implement it.

Review procedure (retrospective)

Take a look at your completed tasks on a regular basis - I suggest you do this on a weekly basis at the most (where possible, also in shorter periods of time) - and see what experiences you have made. What can you learn from it, where do you see concrete possibilities for improvement? Concrete questions for such a review of the procedure could be:

- Which tasks were easy to complete and where were there problems or obstacles? Why?
- Which completed tasks mean a lot to me? (make me proud ...) Why?
- What work did I do too late? Why?
- Which completed tasks have resulted in particularly high benefits / added value? Why?

Based on these - and similar - questions, you can now consider where there is a need for adjustment. Don't take on dozens of measures, but just one or two, which you then really tackle. In this way, you can improve your approach step by step.

Advanced methods in Personal Kanban

As described above, Personal Kanban is not an approach that allows only one specific way of doing things, but a basic framework that allows you to make decisions and adjustments yourself - based on your needs.

In connection with the implementation of Personal Kanban, certain topics arise again and again, which I would like to discuss in more detail below.

Insert more columns

When we add more columns to our basic three-column design, we generally do so for two reasons:

- To include additional cases or situations
- To view and organize the work process in more detail

Let's take a closer look at the most common use cases in the context of Personal Kanban:

Today settle

Many users like to start their day with a brief overview of the tasks they have in mind for the day. To make this clearer, it can be useful to insert another column between the "Backlog" and "In work" columns with the title "Complete today". This column should only contain as many tasks as you really think you can do for the day in question.

In any case, it should be noted that we do not spend 100% of our time on these tasks. In everyday life, there are almost always additional tasks or activities that prevent us from devoting 100% of our time to the implementation of tasks. Phone calls, urgent e-mails, conversations with colleagues, etc. can reduce work performance. A good approach for scheduling the day is about 60% of the available time. If you still have more capacity, you can always take more topics out of the backlog. This way you have a good chance to realize your plans, to be successful with them and to be motivated.

In the evening, you should ideally briefly reflect on the events of the day. Did you achieve your goals? If not - what got in your way? If you find that you are repeatedly or even permanently unable to meet your goals for the day, it makes sense to think about reducing your planning for the day or to look at how, if necessary, existing factors that prevented you from achieving your goals can be reduced.

We will address the issue of unplanned work in more detail in a separate section.

Wait for feedback

It's not always just about feedback. When we perform tasks, there is often a situation where we are waiting for some kind of input from a third party, for example, a callback from a supplier or customer, approval of a concept, or feedback on a proposal. Sometimes there is also the situation that our task is part of a larger process, for example, and we can only continue working on it when another person involved has contributed their part.

If we kept such tasks in our "In Progress" column, we would run the risk of either having to increase WIP limits over time or wait for anyone to have their tasks solved.

In such cases, it can be helpful if we put such tasks in a separate column, which is called "Waiting for feedback" or similar. However, such a column carries the great risk that it becomes a kind of black box and tasks are gradually stacked there and do not evolve. This would not add any value or benefit.

Accordingly, it is important to manage the "Waiting for feedback" column well. It has proven helpful to tag tasks that are pushed into this column with today's date so that you can always track how long the task has been sitting. You should also review the contents daily and take action wherever possible to get the tasks back out of the column. This can be done, for example, by sending a reminder or a request. This way, we can reduce the likelihood of not completing our tasks on time.

Detail the value stream

A third issue that leads us to want to introduce additional columns in our process is often because we want to show the "Doing" or "In Work" column in more detail. This can make sense, for example, if we are working as part of a larger team and there are interfaces to the processes of other participants, or if we do not operate Kanban in the "Personal Kanban" form, but rather run it as a board for a small team, where different work steps should be displayed separately to show bottlenecks and process progress in further detail. The use with Personal Kanban should be considered in each case well. If we assume in Personal Kanban a very small number of tasks, which are parallel in the implementation process, a further subdivision is mostly not purposeful, particularly also, if it concerns a single implementing person and one can assume that these a so limited number of tasks sufficiently well overlooks, in order not to represent the individual status in separate columns to have.

In such a case, it may make more sense to supplement the individual cards with the tasks, for example, with sticky notes or similar, if additional information is to be recorded for a particular task.

Unplanned tasks

Very few people are able to plan all their tasks completely. Time and time again, situations will arise in which existing planning must be adjusted due to changes. In many cases, this happens because new, unplanned tasks suddenly arise or because the prioritization of existing tasks changes. This is what most people experience, and one might ask, somewhat disillusioned, why we should plan at all then, if the plans so often don't hold up. Wouldn't it then make more sense to simply decide and act spontaneously?

In fact, many people act just like that. They see what comes and then make the best of it. Perhaps this has also been your preferred approach up to now. That is probably true at least for a considerable number of the readers of this book. If you act in this way, you run the risk of concentrating so much on the implementation of urgent tasks that the really important things - for example, actively working on your own goals - are pushed into the background and possibly forgotten. We rotate at full speed in the hamster wheel, but we never reach our goal.

Depending on the activity and environment, the amount of unplanned tasks that keep us busy can be larger or smaller. Nevertheless, your goal should be to also work daily on the implementation of important tasks, which can often be planned for the longer term. One approach could be to set a certain amount of "planned tasks" in your planning and schedule the rest for unplanned tasks. This can help you avoid forgetting important things in favor of urgent ones. The appropriate percentage should be determined through trial and error. To do this, it makes sense that you also record unplanned work on your board. This will give you a basis for reviewing and improving your approach in this regard as well. You can better measure the effort based on the corresponding tasks and adjust your planning accordingly.

Ultimately, the transparency of work on unplanned tasks achieved through a board presentation provides another, important benefit. It challenges you to be accountable to yourself. Is it possible that you want to please everyone and therefore always implement every task immediately, questioning too little whether the work is really important? How do you deal with your most valuable asset, your time? Ask yourself whether the tasks you have implemented in the course of the day really justified the effort and were so urgent. Perhaps you could have had more time to implement them and simply scheduled the work. Or maybe you could have talked to the person who created the task early on and worked together to find a way to get it done by someone else.

Question exactly what you spend your time on and think about how you can use your day more beneficially. What you have already done is "over." It's not about feeling bad or guilty for decisions, but solely about understanding what you can do differently, better, in the future and then taking the appropriate action.

Error source Reset work

It happens from time to time that we have to revise our planning due to external circumstances. Tasks that are already in the "In progress" column and on which work has already been started are put on hold in favor of new, more urgent work. In this context, the question now arises how to deal with tasks that have already been worked on, but which are in fact no longer in progress.

Here a clear distinction is necessary: Are we talking about tasks that have been worked on, but which have been postponed based on other priorities, or are we talking about tasks that are no longer to be worked on or are not to be worked on in the foreseeable future due to new tasks? I recommend a pragmatic approach: If the work is only temporarily interrupted and after completion of the more urgent work the originally started work is continued, I recommend a temporary exceeding of the WIP limit. The started task remains in the "In Work" column and will be continued after completion of the additional task. In this case, one should consider whether the planning should be structured in such a way that only a smaller task of the WIP limit is actually actively planned and a part of the capacity is kept free for such unplanned tasks.

If the work started is put on hold and possibly rescheduled, resetting the task is conceivable. In this case, however, it should be clearly noted which part has already been implemented. However, this should be an exception, otherwise the whole planning becomes significantly more difficult and we end up with a situation with many started tasks, which would essentially be the same situation as if we did not limit the WIP values in the "In progress" column. These cases should be considered carefully in any case. Wherever possible, it is worth looking for improvement approaches in the procedure here.

Now there may be cases where work that has already been started suddenly no longer makes sense. It may be that the implementation would come too late and would then no longer bring any benefit. A typical example is the task "Writing Christmas cards", if this task is still in "In progress" in January. Such cards can be removed from the "In Work" column. In any case, I would record them separately and question exactly how the situation came about, and if it is based on mistakes, measures should be sought to ensure that they are not repeated.

Swimlanes and Personal Kanban

You may receive tasks from different sources. Some may come from your professional environment or from customers, others may be tasks that come from the household or family environment. Other tasks may be related to the implementation of your personal or professional goals.

In this case, it may be useful for you to design several swimlanes (swimming lanes) for the different types of tasks, dividing the Kanban board horizontally into several sections:

	To Do / Backlog	Doing / In progress	Done / Done
Professional tasks			
Family tasks			
Tasks from the association			
Tasks to achieve my personal goals			

The tasks of the individual topics are then pushed into the relevant swimlanes and go through the process at this "level".

Of course, it makes sense that you do not set a WIP limit of, for example, "3" for each swimlane, but that the WIP limit affects all swimlanes together. You may want to assign a fixed maximum to a certain swimlane in the process; for example, determine that you set a maximum of one task for the club. However, the sum of the WIP limits of the individual columns should never exceed that of the entire board.

Of course, this approach is not mandatory. But I sometimes find that it helps people keep a better overview of the multitude of different requirements from a wide variety of sources. It's best to find out for yourself what works for you and what doesn't. Draw from the large pool of possibilities.

Story Splitting

I would like to present you an important, extended technique under the keyword "Story Splitting". In fact, this is a term that is mainly used in frameworks and methods for agile product development, where requirements are often formulated in the form of "user stories". Story splitting means that requirements, the aforementioned user stories, are divided into smaller units. This is exactly the approach that we can also take advantage of when implementing tasks and working with OKRs and in Personal Kanban.

The background to this is the fact that tasks that are recorded in the backlog are often very extensive. Imagine you are a student and would like to write a dissertation in order to achieve an academic degree. Now, working on such an assignment covers quite a few different topics. It is about the collection of information, its analysis and evaluation, possibly about own experiments or similar works, which are accomplished, their documentation, the conversion of the appropriate texts, possibly the production of any technical diagrams for the illustration of certain data and much more besides.

If the task "Create dissertation" is now in your backlog, then this task will probably also move to the column "In work" relatively soon, since it is foreseeable that an enormous amount of work will be required here. The task will then remain in this column for the next weeks, months or perhaps even more than a year. This is neither particularly meaningful nor particularly motivating. Rather, it seems a bit like a huge mountain resting on your shoulders.

Right here, another approach would be conceivable: the "Story Splitting". In this way, you could divide the work on the dissertation into small portions, which in turn would make up the entire task in total and which you could transfer individually to the "In progress" column. This would be the basis for working on and completing such small, manageable work packages and thereby drawing lots of motivation from all the tasks that have already been completed. In any case, make sure that the individual work packages do not become too small. It's also no use if you have to draw a new card every few minutes. That would only impair your concentration.

Actually, you could do much more. Probably the creation of the dissertation, or rather the achievement of the associated degree, would be an ideal objective, which in turn would be linked to individual Key Results, from which in turn individual tasks would result. This is exactly where the circle from Personal OKR to Personal Kanban and finally back to OKR closes.

Service classes

But before we now turn to the connection between Personal Kanban and OKRs, let us examine another approach from the Kanban context. It is about service classes. This concept is meant to take into account the fact that there are often tasks of very different urgency and importance. For example, imagine that in a small hospital, the only operating room is scheduled in the morning for a knee joint surgery. The patient has been waiting several days for the operation and today is finally the day. Suddenly, an emergency comes in. Of course, this could be referred to another hospital, but every minute counts. A transfer could have fatal consequences.

Of course, it would be theoretically conceivable to say, "Knee surgery is scheduled today," and refer the emergency patient. But would one really do that? Probably not without an important reason. One would do everything possible to save the life of the emergency patient and postpone the knee surgery, which is not urgent. Both are important operations and the same resources are needed. But the two operations belong in different service classes, as they would say in Kanban. The emergency operation would fall into the class "Urgent" - or, as it is often named in Kanban, "Expedite" - whereas the knee operation would belong to the class "Standard".

This does not refer to the importance of the patient or the desire to do something good for him, but is simply derived from what effect a delay would have. In our case, for one patient it would possibly be the loss of his life, in the other case, according to the doctor's assessment, it would be the inconvenience of the knee patient having to wait an extra day for the procedure and thus possibly having to deal with additional pain.

In the context of Kanban, different service classes are often represented in different swimlanes. Often there is a separate "Expedite Swimlane", which for example is not subject to the WIP limit. What is in this class has the highest priority and is addressed immediately.

In earlier sections, we had talked about urgent orders, for example from the boss. These could be represented in this way, if necessary. Always make sure that the number of "urgent" tasks is really reserved for extreme cases. Otherwise, you will sooner or later find yourself in a situation where you are so absorbed by the urgent tasks that you no longer have time to work on the important ones.

[1] you can also find "work in process" in some books

CHAPTER SEVEN

Combining Personal Kanban and OKRs

You may have wondered why I am combining two such different methods as Personal OKR and Personal Kanban in this book. It might seem that the two are competing and actually just doing the same thing in different ways. That is not entirely true:

When we talk about personnel OKR, we are essentially moving on a strategic level. We are trying to achieve longer-term goals. In the past, the term "strategy" often referred to a time frame of five or ten years, or at least several years. Times have long since changed. In a constantly changing world, in which globalization, rapid technological change, a high degree of complexity and different fashions, approaches, etc. are part of everyday life, the time frame in which we can carry out strategic planning is becoming shorter and shorter. Topics that seemed absolutely central just three years ago may have little significance today or be completely obsolete. Technologies or methods that nobody knew back then may be "state of the art" today.

When we do staff OKR, we are undoubtedly moving at a strategic level. We have seen that there are objectives which may take a year or more to realize, and that we then break them down into smaller units. But even then we are still on the "goal level" and not on the level of concrete activities or tasks. This is exactly where Personal Kanban comes into play.

Personal Kanban can represent the tactical level in interaction with Personal OKR. We deal with which individual activities (tasks) we have to implement in order to achieve the Key Results and in their sum then also address the Objectives. Personal Kanban offers an invaluable advantage. Instead of staying on the level of visions and ideas of goals, we plan concretely the single steps and make them transparent in the context of backlog entries.

Implementing steps is significantly supported by the transparent display on the Kanban board. We can ensure that these topics, which are so important for our further development, do not have to take a back seat in favor of (supposedly) more urgent tasks and are ultimately forgotten.

A good approach is to set concrete implementation tasks based on the key results you have set for achieving the current objectives, which you can then include in the backlog. In this way, you give these objectives more concrete implementation power and can plan the corresponding steps in a very targeted manner. For example, you could schedule a separate swim lane for such tasks and ensure that a WIP limit of "1" is permanently assigned to it from the complete WIP limit that you have used for implementation. In this way, the implementation of your specific goals remains permanently in the current workspace and is implemented step by step.

CHAPTER EIGHT

Implement your OKRs

In my work with individuals, teams, and entire companies on agile topics, I often encounter an unexpected adversary that keeps teams from becoming successful with the techniques, methods, and frameworks taught. To make sure this doesn't happen to the readers of this book, I want to share this important chapter with you. It contains the absolute most important information in the entire book.

Many people have the urge - which for many still stems from their school days - to start with things only when they are sure that they have really understood everything and know all aspects. For some, this means that they don't even start; others waste a lot of time trying to understand and be able to do everything exactly.

At this point, I would like to invite you not to fall into this trap. It may well be that you still have questions after reading the book once or possibly reading the text a second time in order to use it to answer important questions. Don't fall into this trap ... do the most important thing you can do if you want to change something: start! It's not so bad if you don't do everything right in the beginning. You will gain experience and can then look back and see where there is a need for adjustment, because one or the other thing may not have worked as you had hoped. Or you can specifically read through one or the other chapter again, but only when concrete questions arise.

In any case, it is important to start! Only when you start with the implementation, you will find out where there are still questions, or possibly questions, which you have now on a theoretical level, will be clarified when you tackle things concretely.

An important second step is to look at what you have achieved, evaluate the results and decide on one or two improvement topics that you can implement within a small time frame. For this purpose, set a time frame and look at what has changed after its expiration, and then again decide what needs to be done and so on.

Afterword

Many of us have the desire to achieve certain goals. These may come from a professional, personal, family or other context. Opportunities abound. Nevertheless, we often give them away. This happens in the majority of cases not because we have another, more important or more attractive goal, nor because we are lazy. Many of us are very diligent and work really hard. Nevertheless, success eludes us completely or at least partially. In most cases, this is not due to a lack of ability, but because we do not choose the appropriate approaches to achieve our goals.

The combination of Personal OKR and Personal Kanban has continuously brought me forward over the last years. It has led me to my professional independence, helped me to successfully implement various professional and private projects - not least in writing this book.

The beauty of this combination is that it does not require genius or heroic deeds, but can be used successfully by anyone at any time. The only prerequisite is a little bit of discipline, but the methods provide us with additional support. Anyone can do it: so can <u>you</u>.

Why do you only want to dream about goals and their fulfillment? Go for it. Today! Take the first step towards your success and the realization of your very personal goals.

Note

www.ingramcontent.com/pod-product-compliance
Lightning Source LLC
Chambersburg PA
CBHW021140130726
47988CB00003B/1391